THE SECRET: NATURE REVEALS

A COLLECTION OF PURELY EXPRESSED HEART FEELINGS AND VEHEMENCE

HRISHIKESH GOSWAMI

Dedicated to my Parents, Brother, Grandparents and

Teachers.

Contents

Foreword   *xi*

Preface   *xiii*

Acknowledgements   *xv*

NATURE BASED

  1. Nature Reveals   3

  2. Sobbing Beside Mansarovar   4

  3. The Fig Tree   5

  4. The Monsoon Rains   6

  5. My Forbearing Branch   7

  6. Tea   8

  7. Winds Hug The Leaves   9

  8. The Gorgeous Summer   10

  9. O! The Fragrant Of The Jasmine Will Make You Sick   11

10. Nature Was Yours!   12

11. Spring Trees   13

12. Panemorfi Vicinity   14

13. Morning Dew   15

14. The Eternal Leaf   16

15. I Live In A Place Where Birds Sing Alongside Factories Yell   17

16. Underneath These Rocks   18

17. Why Do You Bifurcate?   19

18. Now She Opens Her Mouth   20

19. Ripples   21

20. Aquatic Of While   22

21. Nothing Much Of Trees   23

22. Rain On The Rope   24

Contents

23. Earth Day   25

24. Tree On My Roof   26

25. Climber In My Balcony   27

26. Beach Can Teach You Many   28

27. Seasons   29

28. Amidst The Fork   30

29. The Unsung Father   31

30. Cohere The Water Rise   32

31. The Little Insect   34

32. Who Built This Universe?   35

33. Illogical Misunderstanding   36

34. The Mysterious Cave (part 1)   37

35. The Mysterious Cave (part 2)   38

36. A Bizarre Night (special Mention)   40

37. What Does The Flower Teaches?   41

38. Cosmic Rays   43

39. Captivating Aurora   44

40. The Secret: Nature Reveals   45

41. The Night Is Brief   48

NON- NATURE BASED

42. He Wrote A Romance   51

43. The Carriage That Loped!   52

44. What Can You Expect From The Poet?   53

45. All Things Die   54

46. Strain   55

47. Egotistic   56

Contents

48. Helpful	57
49. Viola	58
50. The Cryptic Circus	59
51. Maria And Joe	60
52. There Was A Day	61
53. Turmoil	63
54. When Life Came To A Standstill	64
55. Life In A Boat	65
56. Extraordinary Feats	67
57. Poets Are Many	69
58. Who Is A Poet?	71
59. Everyday Is A New Challenge For Me	72
60. Extreme Destitution	74
61. I Will Perish Them Away	75
62. Failure Comes Quicker Than Success	76
63. Your Hands	77
64. Love Rose	78
65. Trust	79
66. Your Home	80
67. Injustice	81
68. Death After Death	82
69. Whom Did I Say?	83
70. Linctus May Not Heal	85
71. What Hurts You Most?	86
72. I Can Never Be A Poet	87
73. My Poem	88

Contents

74. Mixed	89
75. My Today's Day	90
76. Nothing Goes Round	91
77. Poetry In His Mind	92
78. Am I Fragile?	93
79. Life Has Taken A Turn	94
80. And Now I Know	95
81. Who Am I?	96
82. Nonsense Creation	98
83. Eyes That Feel	99
84. Harnessing The Misfortunes	100
85. In The Sea Of Time	101
86. Confused Teen	102
87. A Dry Poem	103
88. Time -time -time!	104
89. Never Ending Race To Success!	105
90. Fairyland	106
91. I Missed It	107
92. Why Are We So Indolent?	109
93. Wicked Things Approach	110
94. How The Diya Glimmers And Offs!	111

MISCELLANEOUS

95. The Goddess Of War	115
96. Krishna	116
97. Stunning Diwali Isn't?	117
98. Christmas	118

Contents

99. New Year Poem — 119

100. Pen Pencil And So — 120

101. Wordsworth Frost And Shelly — 121

102. The Ahoms Of Assam — 123

103. A Robust Women — 124

104. Holi — 125

105. Not Ever Ending Jet — 126

106. Granny's Pond — 127

107. Science And Literature — 128

108. Bihu — 129

109. Jules Verne — 130

110. Robert Frost — 131

111. Isaac Newton — 132

112. My Grandfather — 133

113. My Grandmother — 134

114. Workers Are Not Only Workers — 135

115. Tutankhamun — 136

PROSE

116. Time: A New Chapter — 139

117. What Is Smart Work? — 140

118. Idle Brain: Devil's Workshop — 141

119. World No Tobacco Day — 142

QUOTES

120. Quotes — 145

121. Comments On Poetry — 146

122. Critical Analysis — 148

Contents

E- PLATFORMS

123. Youtube   151

124. Links To All Other Platforms   152

About The Poet   153

Foreword

Dear Hrishikesh,

Going through your poems, I felt a passionate poet in you. Your pent up feelings beautifully brings out the serious verse-maker inside you. I wish you all success in life. Keep writing what your heart desires via verse!

Best wishes as always!

-Saikh Md. Sabah Al-Ahmed
Winner of the Reuel International Prize for Poetry
(2019)

These poems are the spontaneous outpouring of a highly reflective mind and a profoundly sensitive soul. It should be nurtured to give even more delight to the discerning reader.

-Shobha Bora
Senior Teacher of English
Don Bosco High Sec. School
Panbazar, Guwahati 781001

Your poems are truly appreciative. Keep up your good works. I enjoyed your poems.

-Kasturi Devi
Teacher of English
Sai Rns Academy
Kahilipara, Guwahati 781019

Preface

Poet: "How are you, my dear?"

Nature: "I am shedding tears from morn till eve…"

Poet: "And what has caused the Nature to shed tears?"

Nature: "No one beckons me to the ever rising civilization and so for…"

Poet: "I shall beckon you to my monumental elusive heart"

Nature: "And what's the worth?"

Poet: "Give me thoughts and imagination and this will work."

Nature: "I promise to reveal the secrets to you…"

Poet: "I shall be waiting for you Panemorfi Vicinity!"

Nature: "Let us unruffled motivate the human race and see what upshot they acquire at the end of this manuscript."

Poet: Dear readers,

I am a retainer of nature and after my "Poet's Words", I have become a retainer of mankind to. I welcome you all to join me in this audacious journey of Nature and man and help me underline the secrets that the Nature has just now promised to reveal and yes do remember, 'In the space between writer and **reader** *is the* **poem**. *It is where the writer and* **reader** *exchange, like breathing. The writer breathes out, the* **reader** *breathes in,*

the **reader** *breathes out, and the writer breathes in again.'*

Acknowledgements

I am quite glad that I have at last succeeded to cope up along with all the encumbrances, the task of successfully fetching this piece out for my dear readers, who are quite excited to dip into the strings of verses, phrases and words, savor the taste of feelings and relish the honey of poetry of all genre in just one go. It was not a piece of cake for me to draft out all the sentiments in a fragment of sentences and in every instance a crack or crevice used to appear which again desired to be healed.

Nevertheless I would like to take the time, to thank Mr. Saikh Md. Sabah Al-Ahmed, Winner of the Reuel International Prize for Poetry (2019) for serenely reading my poems and drafting me the most honest reply. He also stood beside me during my first venture, "Poet's Words". Thank You Sir!

I would at the same time thank Mrs. Shobha Bora and Mrs. Kasturi Devi for guiding me and providing me with their priceless time and rejoinder. They have been my English teachers and an endless source of impetus for me. Thank you so much teachers!

No work is possible without the sustenance of family, friends and well-wishers. Therefore I would like to whole heartedly thank my parents Dr. Anjan Goswami (Father) and Mrs. Pallabi Goswami (Mother) along with Mr. Mahendra Goswami (Grandfather), Mrs. Pori Goswami (Grandmother) and Mrs. Manoroma Goswami (Maternal Grandmother) for constantly standing by my side when I aspired them the most.

Lastly I would take the time to thank all my near and dear once and my School and Allen faculties for always making me feel sturdy and ratified.

-Hrishikesh Goswami

India Book of Records Holder

Recipient of India Prime Top 100 Author Award 2022

Recipient of India Star Icon Award 2022

NATURE BASED

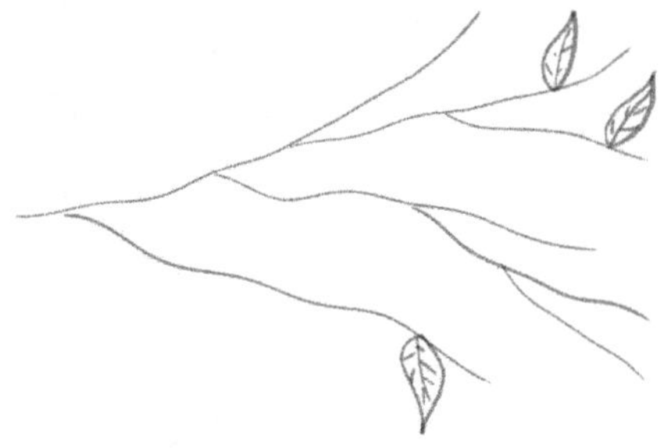

1. Nature Reveals

(Published in the Assam Tribune)
(Fetched Poem of the Week Award)
(Fetched Creative Endeavour of the Month)
The rocks on which I am sitting are
Made of gold.
They do not belong to me
Nor to you...
However, they belong to
Both of us.
We are natures
Creations and
Not creators
We should curb ourselves
To our finger nails
Because a long nail
Is prone to break.

2. Sobbing Beside Mansarovar

Who can get out the charm?
The belle of the chilled
Glacial waters of heavenly sapphire
Love dipped, sanctity filled Mansarovar...
I sat beside them
Which impervious to express
Like the occult hallucinations of one
Compelled me to sob
To cry beside the waters
Not on my sins
However, on my known viles.

3. The Fig Tree

And who the bushy cover
Felon over the ground
Draining nutrition and reserves
Out of the muddy cover
No response from ground
Oh my dear mother you are great
To all your children
The fig tree grows nourishing us
Supplying victuals and refuge to birds
Those birds are not quite big
To understand the importance of the fig
And the fig is quite big
To understand the vitality Of the soil!

4. The Monsoon Rains

You promised to visit me, isn't it?
My dear
When the sky was black
And clouds were poignant about
You came like vehemence to me
Making me write your very presence
You are marvelous at swindling
Get your way to the farmers' fields
Who are right now crying?
On their fortune and preparing
To live the hamlet
Go Monsoon Rains go!!

5. My Forbearing Branch

O! My forbearing branch

My hale and hearty little feat

You bear the burden of leaves

And the load of birds

Without grouching the same

You taught me to be happy at the cheerless moment

And sad at the joyous moment

I see you every morning

Lingering and praying

To Him about the same.....

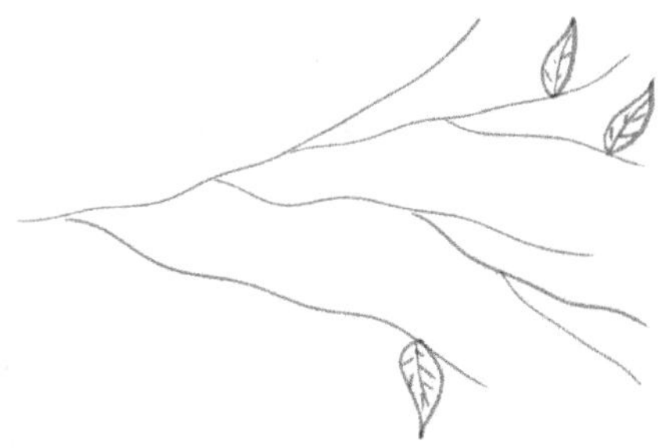

6. Tea

(Published in the Assam Tribune)
How astounding how yummy
Is the tea
Of Assam!!
I enjoy it with
Adore, enthusiasm and delight.
I love to sip
And carve up a cup of tea
Every morn and every eve
There are some petals
And some flowers
In my kitchen garden
Which fail to be a magnet for
Me as much as the tea.

7. Winds Hug the Leaves

(Published in the Horizon)
Yesterday, 22nd September
I saw few
Adolescent olive plants
O! They were dazzling
Like gold and emerald
In the yellow September sunlight
I love the orange!
I love the light!
Winds hug the leaves
Causing it to move
Left Right and left again
My biro flew down
This lean folio like the
Unstoppable September Sun
My September my nativity my day...

8. The Gorgeous Summer

I was pretending to sleep
On my lofty fluffy bed
Since I didn't want to get up early
But you know the summer
It's so melting
Once and for all
I jumped out of my bed
Not able to defy the heat
Someday I may get a dub
From a noble man
Regarding my exertion
On this gorgeous summer morning.

9. O! The Fragrant of The Jasmine will make you Sick

O! The fragrant of the jasmine will make you sick

So brawny so pretending

Falling in love with the nightly sky

I was transiting by the corner

Pondering upon my selfish deeds

When it made me realize...

Nothing last for long (2)

It goes on!

10. Nature was Yours!

You heard it right

Nature was yours

But now it's no more

You plunk in the halfway

Flanked by possessing and leaving it off

You are a critical person

Who reads Nature in my verse?

And in your

School textbooks

But Abandon it in Reality

You can be precious to your contiguous one

But Nature is closer to all

Leave this game

And commence a noble life

With sky as your roof

Grass cot as your floor

And Forest as your plane walls.

11. Spring Trees

The trees aren't that good-looking this morning
They are lofty, brawny and stuffy
My minds in reverting from them
I need a counselor, go get it
"Spring it not for me",
Said she
I was astounded at this
When I found myself staring at the spring trees
Outside the casement casing.

12. Panemorfi Vicinity

O! The little Panemorfi Vicinity
The little ideal place of mine
You are lauded with shake and twigs
For you house free birds and novice animals
You house the mighty sun
And the Prodigious river
You are not only a place but also a
Panemorfi thought
I love thinking and dreaming about you
Please return to this originally duplicate world
I shall be waiting for you...

13. Morning Dew

The pathetic scene
I saw today
Touched me impassive
The herbs on the precincts floor
Bore the weight of dew drops
A sensitivity or chillness ran from top to toe
Intensely shaken with angst
I decided to pen down something
Irrespective of what others may say
Conceivably I may not get to perceive
Such a thespian sight again in this life.
What did the Nature Reveal? (3)

14. The Eternal Leaf

15. I Live in a Place where Birds Sing Alongside Factories Yell

I live in a place where birds sing alongside factories yell,
I live in a place where spotless and reeking water meets,
In a place where people contemplate and swill;
I live in a place where people sentient and perish;
In a place where sun sheens with volley,
I live in a place where people toss and plead,
I live in a place where people clairvoyant and lie.

16. Underneath These Rocks

Underneath these rocks
I sat one day
Determining about my forthcoming
When a sparrow fluttered down;
The only mock hutment
And spilled upon me
A dozen blessings.

17. Why do You Bifurcate?

I am the inquirer
And she is the respondent
O dear
Why do you bifurcate?
Split your branches?
To which she retorted
I am the lonesome traveler
Just like you
But disparate you
I can palate both the ways
And then tell with a mark
I am far more adept
That you are!

18. Now She Opens Her Mouth

Showery night,
Blustery trees
Branching directions
To the house of ripostes
I found her deskbound beside a slab
Keeping down her judgments
On a reedy slip of tabloid
What are you scripting?
To which came an open mouth
Full of blues and agony
I can't pronounce.

19. Ripples

The ripples of the rain drops
Make me feel healthy,
Out of slumber and
Full of spirit.

20. Aquatic of While

The aquatic of while is full of syrupy linctus
But of course
I can't sojourn
Sojourn here and go to the same
Sequestered isle to unwind
And occupy my spell within.

21. Nothing Much of Trees

The world is plummeting
Out of envy and jealously.
The oxygen I give verves to the beast,
The primates without tails
And the lions without claws.
I am the wax light of optimism for them
I am the chaperon of them
Headed for a lively future
But nothing much of 'me'. (2)

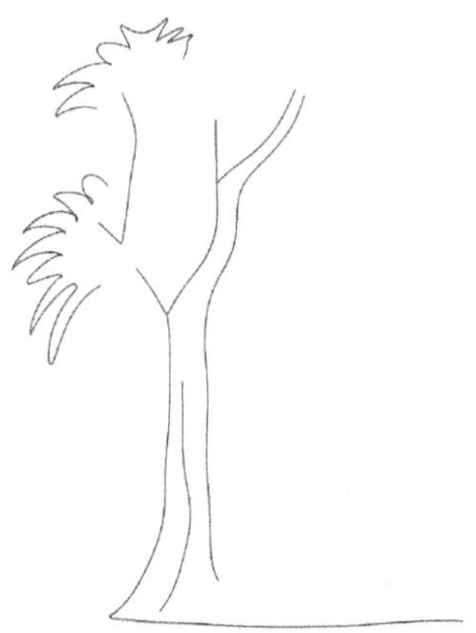

22. Rain on the Rope

The icy drips of liquid
On the cloth line
Banged against my face.
The cubicles of my body
Became turgid and busted out their love
To all the flesh of this physique.
The rain on the rope
Made me wistful about my juvenile days.

23. Earth Day

Every day is an unfamiliar day for me
For it brings me the thought of my Mother
She feeds me with yields, tubers and berries.
Nourishing me with water and garden-fresh air
Providing me contentment and opulence
In every aspect of my life.
She supports me with her two hands
Empowering me to sit on them
When I am demoralized and tumble-down
By some shadowy forces
But now this very dark force
Is seizing my mother
I am afraid
That in the near future or so
They will shamble her life
And also theirs!

24. Tree on My Roof

The tree on my roof

It's not as lanky as you think

It is like a hook

That plays the play birds

And line the blameless parasites

It is a home-grown to bugs and

A revelry spot for birds

It is also the onlooker

Of numerous volley and sleet storms.

25. Climber in My Balcony

The climber in my balcony

Was once inland

It was not thriving

The way it should

So I

Let it break alfresco

Not for a month

That it has achieve thrice its size.

26. Beach can Teach You Many

The beach teaches you
To reconcile up the gashes
Made by others feet
With the help of the waters
It teaches you to clean
Yourself every time you are
Beleaguered by many.

27. Seasons

Why do you wait?
Wait for the next season
Season will change
Times will vary
You howl at summer
And neglect winter
You want fervor at hatred
And hatred at fervor.
Why is it so?
Can't you enjoy?
This very present
This very season
This very moment?

28. Amidst the Fork

Yesterday I sat
Between the arms of
My loving mother,
The tree!
O tree!
Fail to realize
I sat unaltered untarnished
In addition, do you know
What I saw?!
The sun was trying to
Lug the waters of the tarn
Amidst which
Was I and you together.

29. The Unsung Father

(Published in the Horizon)
Long ago it commenced
This is the chronicle that reflects the
Fine lines of the unsung
The bright blue and
The vast sizable figure
With neither beard nor moustache
The heart of whose goes beyond the
Emerald blue and orange sea
It hovers on top of your temple
Day in and day out
But you break to grasp its panjandrum
Unless and until a flying utensil
Passes off whose clatter is ample
To turn your head at least once
Towards the father figure,
The protector, the 'sky'!

30. COHERE THE WATER RISE

(Published in the 10ᵗʰ Anniversary of Bow Seat Ocean Awareness
Program)
Cohere the water rising
Prevent it from butchering
The gorgeous things of the marine
The corals, fishes, and sea lions,
The penguins, walruses and polar bears.
It will escalate by another...
Another 1.4°C or 5.8°C
By the end of this century
It has given a boost to
Water disasters and calamities
Like hurricanes, droughts, and climate change!
The coastal areas are worst hit
It makes the river wobbly and
The ocean sops up surfeit heat
From greenhouse gas emissions,
Causing to levitate ocean hotness
Thermal expansion of sea water and
Melting of land ice
Ensuing in coral bleaching and trouncing
Of breeding ground for marine fishes.

HRISHIKESH GOSWAMI

Guardians it's high time
Pick up your expertise to impede this melting
Button on to eco-friendly stuff!
And prevent this planet
From changing its pristine colours of blue and green!

31. The Little Insect

Hey the little insect
You are frustrating to peep through
The lattice of the darkest corner
But see
I recognized you
I think we met some day
At a diverse place
Oh! I don't remember it
Perhaps it is you who comprehend
My feelings and is
Selflessly trying to convey it to me
But the dilemma lies in the fact that
I can't let you in
For you are not accepted
Neither welcomed by any
So please draw back
Retreat to your place and live a contented life there
Away from the Madding Crowd.

32. Who Built this Universe?

And who he is
With a procedural mind
And who he is
With great poetic reverbs
And who he is
To create a space for me?
I think I know the answer
But fail to share it
With you dear.
There are many things to ponder
So poignant so alluring
I shall try to explain you one day
Who built this Universe?

33. Illogical Misunderstanding

There has been some sort of
Misunderstanding amid
The poet and the nature
The verses are going hostile to the nature
This is sensibly inacceptable
Stand on! Hold on!
Let's see what the Nature Reveals!
After a decade or a century
I hope to see tomorrow's light
Before I sleep tonight.

34. The Mysterious Cave (Part 1)

The autumn landscape

"Landscape of the soul"

Reminds me of the landscape

Which I now recall goes somewhat like this:

Long ago in the yellow woods

Open was a cave

With all that sapphire

And gold

Gelid opening, nostalgic past and all that.

I sat out my shower

Sneaked through the cave

Botched to realize that once closed

The cave would not unbolt again

This nightmare ran through my veins and blood

I was frightened and gone

Came back my breath when I saw

It was only a Nightmare

It was only a nightmare.

(To be continued...)

35. The Mysterious Cave (Part 2)

Come on come on

Let's set on to the

Mysterious pothole

Yet again this summer

The fables narrated:

Long ago set on the foot hills

A mysterious cave swallowing folks

The ramparts of the cave were stunning

It seemed to open into a new Universe altogether

As you would remember

I was locked inside the cave

I followed the footprints of common men

I was led into ways

"As ways lead onto ways"

I found a golden age

A golden thought Inexpressible in poetry or paintings

I found the honey of literature

My ultimate yearning

Was to allocate this excursion with you dear.

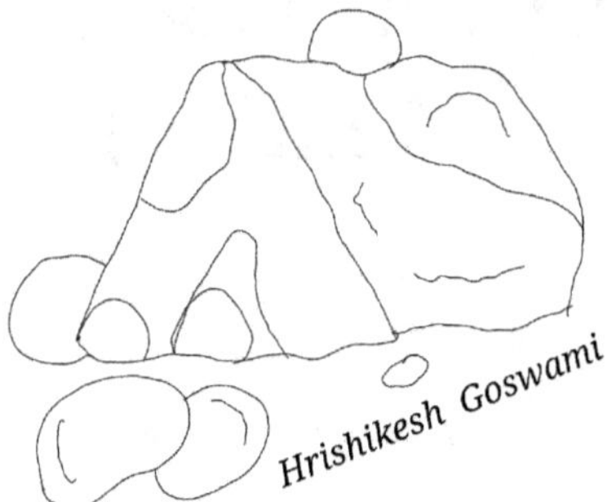
Hrishikesh Goswami

36. A Bizarre Night (Special Mention)

Today's night is particular

It is atypical in the sagacity that

It is quite gloomy tonight

As I run bed ward to glance all through the casement

The bosky and brume backdrop outside

I am unable to deem them in my dell

Dolor has elded my heart

The flexuous bed and fuliginous sky is not capable

To give me a superior troupe

I can hark to sound of the lizard

O yes! I can see the incarnadine

Inhumed under the pillow

Perhaps the welkin is my only swain.

37. What does the Flower Teaches?

The petite sprout
Ages into a fledged flower
Of outsourcing exquisiteness and charisma
It then rips and wilts and
At length meets its fate
Consonantly the mortal body sees its fate
But the soul and the poetic wits
Tend to live on for ever
Inspiring new-fangled works of the alike.
This is what the Flower teaches.

38. Cosmic Rays

Ah! The cosmic rays
Seems to move towards
The soul of mine
For another twenty three light years
I will be back again
Again with another poem.

39. Captivating Aurora

O the polar slant
Of the cosmic sink
You are predominantly seen
On the magnetosphere
Caused by the solar winds
And the captivating breeze
You are out of anyone's reach
For you
Design the soul within.

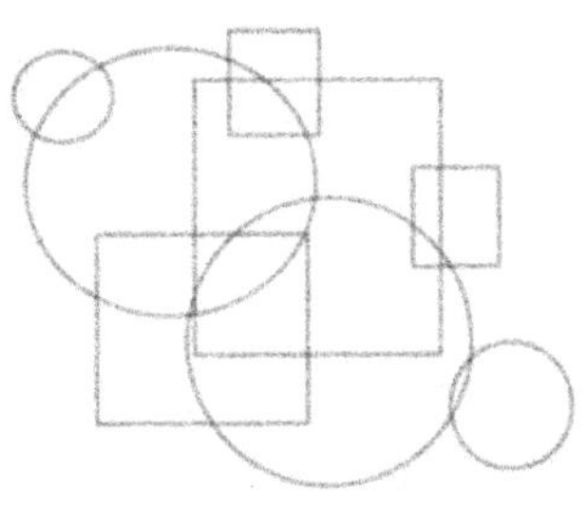

40. The Secret: Nature Reveals

O the secret

The secret which I deciphered

While rifling through the crusty pages of

An old beige book

I enjoyed the flavor

I readily enjoyed the pleasure

Of deciphering the codes of Nature

In the relationship

Between nature and mankind

Nature is at all times the central

But levity permits us to rework the blur vision of mortal

Into a vibrant vision of a procrastinator

Who cheerfully enjoys each and every second

Of his pro time

But gets curbed in Time

And post time

Me, sedentary, underneath the oak

Looking at the slender grasses

Enables me to think;

Something often...

Ignored in the main course of time

And which upshots into conflicts@

Between nature and man.

One who kills nature

Kills himself
In the hirsute wooden branches
Of the banyan
I bargain the mystery of the cave
*And inside the cave**
The honey of Literature. #

*Referring to the poem: <u>The Mysterious Cave (Part 1)</u>
Referring to the poem: <u>The Mysterious Cave (Part 2)</u>
@ Referring to the poem: <u>Illogical Misunderstanding</u>*

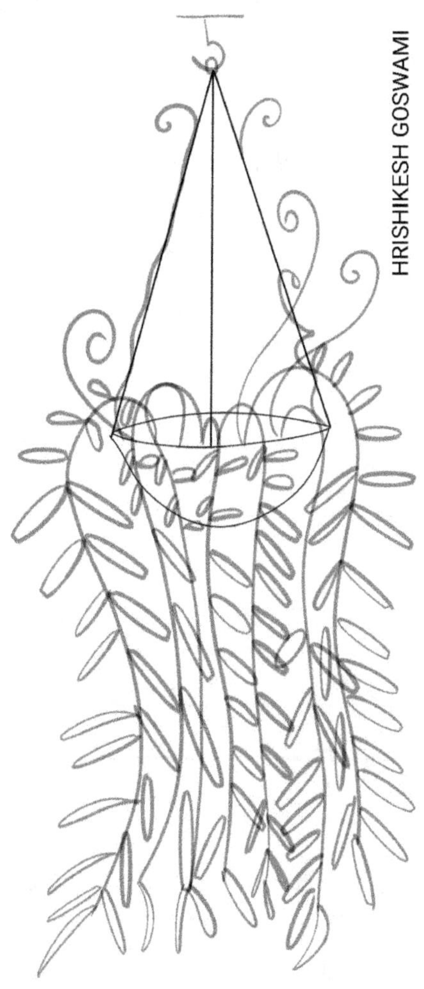

HRISHIKESH GOSWAMI

41. The Night is Brief

The Night is now brief
Too brief to elucidate.
I shall perish tomorrow...

NON- NATURE BASED

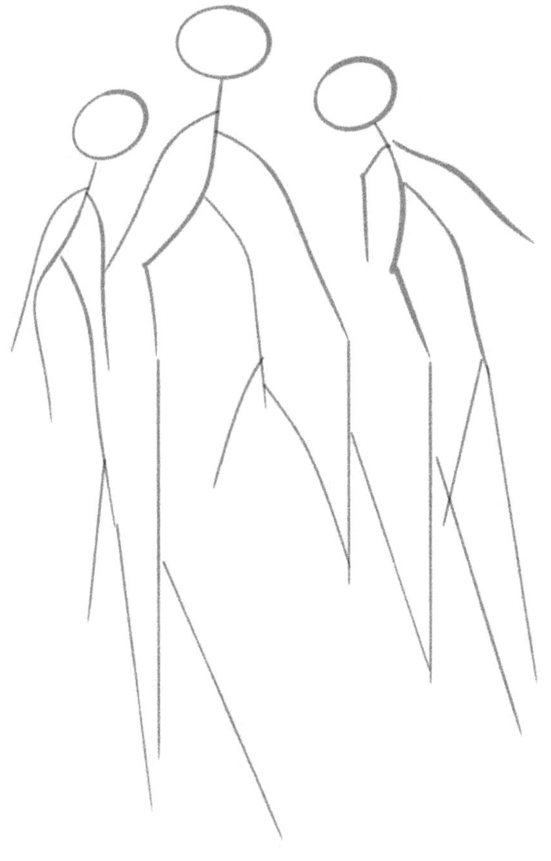

42. He Wrote a Romance

I saw him lettering
The other day
Fixed to his desk with the coop
On his left
Folio on his right
He was weaving axioms out of feelings
Meditative and tranquil
For me to appreciate
He was cooking Romance.

43. The Carriage That Loped!

(Shortest poem of Hrishikesh Goswami)
The carriage that loped like a jet now siestas in cease-fire.

44. What can you Expect from the Poet?

The poet
Is deafened for the physical noises
He is unsighted for the factual colours,
He is dumb for the exposed politics
And hypocrisy
So what do you expect from the Poet?

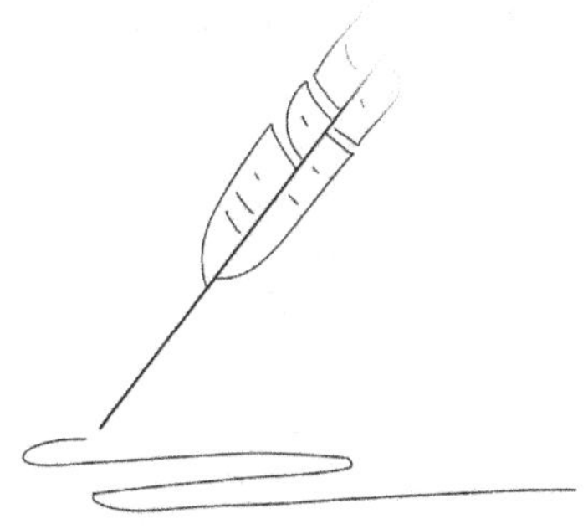

45. All Things Die

There is nonentity fresh
In this era timeworn notion but yes
There is many things to learn from the same
You may be mislaid by the egotistical world
But the fear of death
Will seldom guide you through the precise trail
My acquaintance
You are not less than a mortal like me
But always retain this in cognizance
Every summer ends when
The first autumn leaf falls!

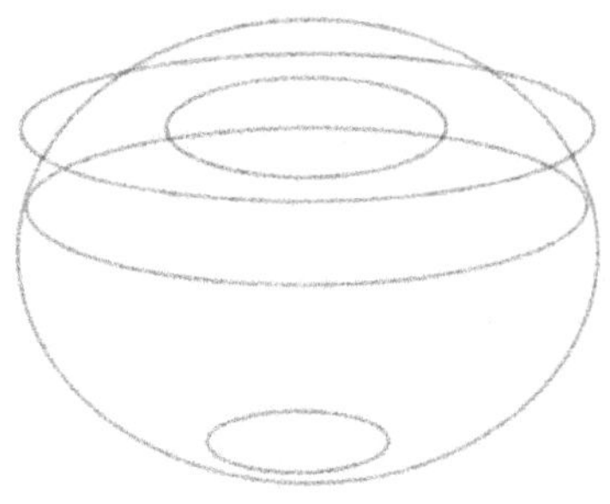

46. Strain

The strain on the leaf
Gives me a strain
On my face when
I was observing it
Not with my eyes
But with my heart.

47. Egotistic

The egotistic lady
Fails to appreciate the charisma
And beauty of bequests.
She is stupefied
By her egotistical milieu.
She perceives all to be like her.
She ruminates of her to possess
Many erratic jewels which
In other words
Should always
Stay with her lifelong.
But lady you must fathom
That zilch last for long
It goes on.

48. Helpful

He was a man of virtue
A very helpful being.
The fellow aids others
And say may I see
A person who can
Fathom well and
Not cross query my
Questions about
Kindness and bounteousness.

49. Viola

The viola of western colours
Sang a wise tone right on my face.
I was obliged to ruminate about the same.
Viola of colours
Thin body
Broad end
And an impressive smile
Singing the old Vikings
And giving a cryptic look to my limericks.

50. The Cryptic Circus

This was the circus
You would love to visit
It was lauded with smiles and joy
Colours and mischiefs
My life was no less than a spectacle
Of pale and lively colours
High and low pitches
Loud and soft voices.

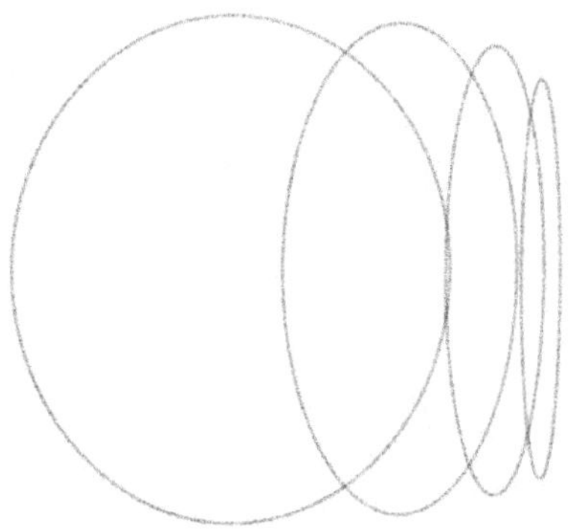

51. Maria and Joe

The Sun shined cripplingly
On the couple
Booming a bag with them
They were Maria and Joe
Maria was seven and Joe ten
Life might someday take a total gyration
If the novelist
Coveted to host
A melody not known by many
And crooned by none.

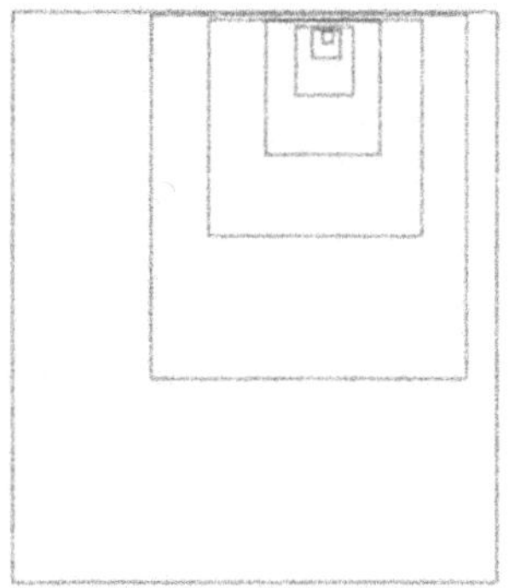

52. There was a Day

There was a day
When I had none
And now that
I have had it all
It becomes an ordinary for me
One which was once exquisite
Now becomes a mere
Piece of liability.

53. Turmoil

The state of affairs is tensed

Ubiquitous screams and clamor

Life is susceptible to extermination

Manhood will now not curlicue

The turmoil of this microbe

Has dwindled us

Of all our armaments

And is now wounding

Us intellectually and materially.

54. When Life Came to a Standstill

I roused up in the daybreak
It was silence silences
All around
Not a timid leaf ventured to
Leave its branch
The asphalt seemed unused
For years
Life came to a standstill.

55. Life in a Boat

(Critically Analysed by Fruit Journal, Manchester (UK))
Life in a boat
Looks romantic,
From the neighboring island.
Similarly life in the island
Seems artless and laid-back
From the boat.
The sailor thinks of halting
While the halter thinks of sailing;
Both are a mere piece of
Illusion to each other.

Hrishikesh Goswami

56. Extraordinary Feats

Neruda was a poet
Einstein was a scientist
Bhupen da was a vocalist
Bezbaruah was an author
They had proficiencies
Similar to us
But used them extraordinarily
To achieve extraordinary feats.

57. Poets are Many

It's true that
Poets are many
They may be lovers,
Haters, inventers or slayers.
But I am none of those
I am a goalless ray
Of the full moon night,
I am the bridge bond
Of some anonymous hydrogen.

Hrishikesh Goswami

58. Who is a Poet?

(Critically Analysed by Fruit Journal, Manchester (UK))

Poet is he who
Transcribed this verse
He who saw the nature
He who touched the sky
He who felt the birds
He who heard the river
He who tasted this Earth

59. Everyday is a New Challenge for Me

(Critically Analysed by Fruit Journal, Manchester (UK))
Now everyday is a challenge
A hard-hitting task to accomplish
Morning gives me a parcel of works
Evening ceases my cognizance from me
And night…
What to say?!
Takes away my kip.
But encounters are what makes life interesting
Appending them gives me pleasure
Overshadowing them gives me eternal happiness.

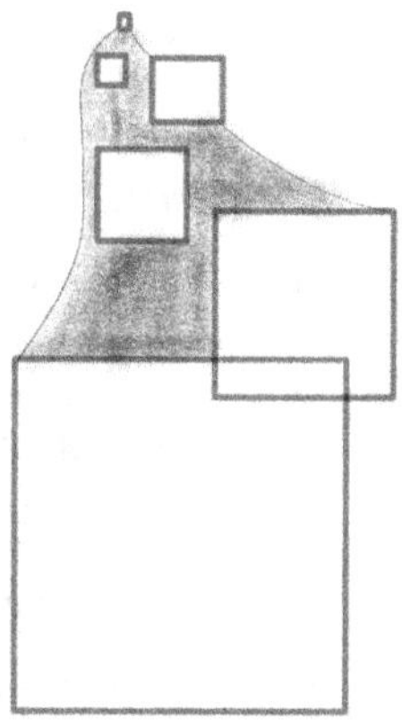

60. Extreme Destitution

The nature's clouts

Stabs to make us sense

Her occurrence

Again and again

Yet again

Rumbling gales, shattering typhoons,

And life intimidating seismic activity

Mark us exceptionally anxious

About our breathes and there after

Lies a plethora of secrets

Yet to come,

Will blew us black and blue

Nostalgic about the noble timeworn days

I will someday make this

Turn into imagination from reality!

But up till than

We will have to writhe

Extreme hardship

And extreme hardship.

61. I Will Perish Them Away

I will perish them away
All away dejected in hell,
You will be blown off
From my land
You interlopers,
You traitors,
You forlorn, self-seeking mortals
Dragon merry cake
Someone will slay you
Slay you in the dungeon
And nail you in the custodial.
The obscure cells will eat you raw
In the filthy murky ways
You polluted me.

62. Failure Comes Quicker than Success

You may wonder
What I say!
You may analyse and
Pore over all that
You perceive all that I express
But I am a mere expresser
I am a lover of nature and
Today tell you
Failure comes quicker than success.
Failure will harm you
Both internally and externally
If you don't sojourn it
From confronting you
Every ninth time which
Heralds your tenth success.

63. Your Hands

Don't you reason
You are too silly
To not use your hands
When you must
You who love sedentary
And telling things
Extrovert you people
Fail to appreciate the
Introvertedness of your hands.
They are exquisite not only to you
But for me too
You wonder why?
Which I shall tell you another day.

64. Love Rose

The rose you love
And the love that rose possess
Are synergistic in the sense that
The more you chase it,
The harder it is to catch.

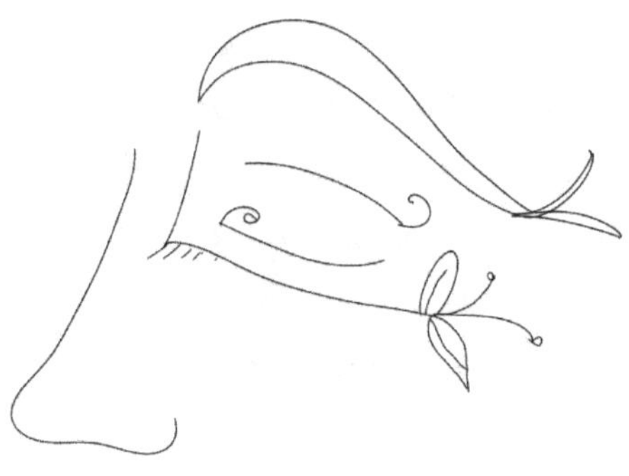

65. Trust

Trust can be broken
Like a delicate glass
But cannot be secured again.

66. Your Home

Your home
Ought to be the center
And not the fringe
Of your affection.

67. Injustice

Injustice anywhere
Is a threat to justice everywhere
An artless act of injustice
Can collapse the entire uprightness
Of a tribe
It can shamble the doppelgänger
Of an elapsed ruler.

68. Death After Death

One who proficiencies death
Not once but twice
Is a pity drawer
He holds the talent
To latch the eye of the
One who have not
Experienced it at least once
And conceivably he will touch
Many deaths.

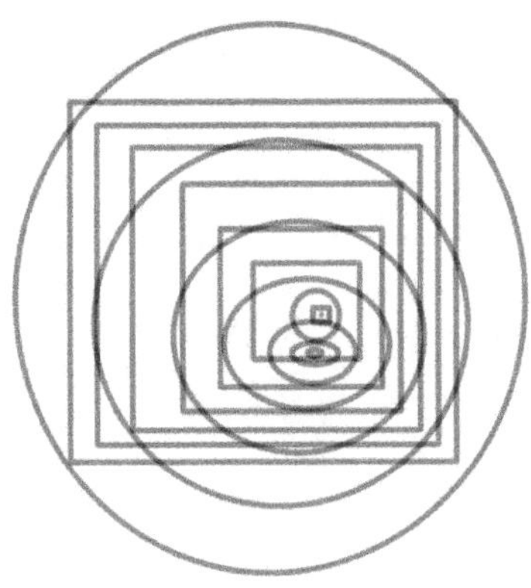

69. Whom did I say?

Whom did I say?
About my intact life.
It is you
O! You know me
Through my verses
Through my write ups
You now own all the authority to
Tear off the pages of
My life.

Hrishikesh Goswami

70. Linctus May Not Heal

Linctus may not heal
The lesions made by words,
And words may not heal the
Lesions made with poems.

71. What Hurts You Most?

What hurts you most?
Day after day
Night after night
Is it the light?
Or is it the darkness?
Or is it the word?

72. I Can Never Be a Poet

73. My Poem

I am a child
Running about like an unwise frog
Climbing on the rocks and stones
Dancing like a goldfinch
Yelling like a wolf
Leaping like a panther
In the yellow commons
Of my mother.
I grew
Got uninterested with about nothing to do,
And then unexpectedly the whole shebang
One day transformed
I saw a peer of mine
Sitting and not worsening
An ounce of his worthy
I took to construing
And lettering followed
Not at all
Realizing the importance of study
I now recall my childhood days
While making for a tougher day
Which I shall now
Along all face
And set to go about with another day.

74. Mixed

Everything is mixed,
Mixed in the sense that
They fail to satisfy
Someone's innermost urge for imbibing
The diet of the poor
Comes like the judgments to the scripter
It is scarce and narrow,
Narrow in the sense that
It fails to keep the readers
Unbroken for eras together
Even the Nature now shows,
Shows me mixed concepts
Of ecstasy and audacity
I am a coward
Fixed behind the bars,
Bars not of brace
But of mere misfortunes
Mixed is my life
And that of yours
Because we live in world
Of Mixed...

75. My Today's Day

It was an audacious day
I went about with Holmes's Lens
Fetching goodies for my own
Nursing my empty pot
I now slumber less
And slog more
I am circumscribed by someone
Averting by wingspan
I can't stand on my bare legs
My eyes are crumpling
Like the leaf of an autumn birch
I can now reminiscence the morning
When I primed the tea
For myself
And now as I sit
Dying on my own deeds.

76. Nothing Goes Round

Nothing goes roundabout
I say
As I aspire myself
Back to the Colosseum
Living to eat like a dandy fellow
Joker at the Grand Canyon
I can never stay aback
To see what my feats achieved.

77. Poetry in His Mind

I read his mind one day
"Poetry it is",
She says
I know that by some other day
But he now says
I have something in my mind
But no home to express,
No melody to set-up,
No single to eavesdrop.
I then advised him
To visit the bordering forest
Now deskbound to his study
He carved a novel
Which I now call 'A Poetry in His Mind'.

78. Am I Fragile?

Am I fragile or am I not
This wholly depends on
How you perceive me;
And how your judgments perceive me
I can be a boulder;
Or simply a paper;
But always remember
There is a hidden fire within… (2)

79. Life Has Taken a Turn

The year was 2019
I was not to be mentioned
A lover of the lovers
I sat down in the amphitheater
Inspecting the furious of all men
Bout with each other
An unexpected thought ran down my spine
I quickly hopped and slipped
From where I sat
Hastened across the archive
Then the Head's Bureau;
And then my eyes felt on a volume
Which I now recall
Gave me the spirit to engrave;
And the wisdom to reason
I overlooking all discomforts of life
Began to relish the extant
As never before
Not to be mentioned
I was in the ninth;
And my life had taken a turn.

80. And Now I Know

(This very poem contains all the letters of the English alphabet.)
Yesterday I saw a dog howling and
Jumping over the fence of exact wood
Unsolicited, unwanted
A lotus in the mid pond
I ran like the blowing zephyr;
And flushed across the doors of temple
I tempted to see a bigger picture
Of my questioning name.

81. Who am I?

I think I know
From quite a long time
Who am not I?
17 years have conceded
And I still don't know
Who am I!
I may be a sailor
Cruising in the Atlantic
Or a seaman
Loading the pirate's deck
But I am not
I may be a tree
Standing still amidst the swards
But I know,
I am not
Then pal who am I?
Am I a vocalist?
Am I a novelist?
Or am I a poet?
17 years have conceded And the answer still….
I am none of them
I am a fragment of the broken second
I am an historic piece from an antique stone
I am a piece from Mother Nature

I am a deviated ray from the mighty sun.
And so you can't describe me
As one amidst you all.

• 97 •

82. Nonsense Creation

Who underway the creation of this historic landscape?
Full of mystery young men
I myself cross questioned myself
And got an answer
Straight from overhead
This is I me myself
I asked
Who are you dear?
He replied in passive
I am your fate
You will be a maker
Of an antique landscape
And one day a boy of 17
Will question you the same…
So dear who is the nonsense creator?
And who is the actual protagonist?

83. Eyes that Feel

I am a mischievous kid
Who not realizing the second
Jumps into the loop
Of waves and light
I nous them with my pair of eyes
I yelp with them
I lookout the fowls and saplings with them
But I can also feel with them
I can tell if your heart
Is soft or not!
If your behavior
Is pleasing or peeving
All in a go with them.

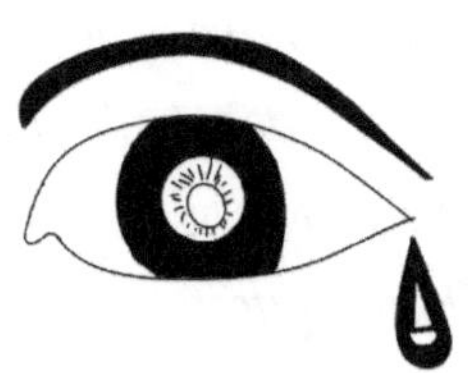

84. Harnessing the Misfortunes

I have started harnessing some of my
Misfortunes into Fortunes of Tomorrow
But there still lies certain lacunas in me
Which avert me from doing so
Yesterday when the world was slumbering
I was awake, alert and abrupt
Like the alligator of some tropical land
I am a vessel of the Pacific
Which tends to float erratically throughout its Journey
I am the moon
Which can only imitate someone
Else's light
And I am a mere piece of lad
Who after waning to do good work
Goes into the awe of failure and so…
Isn't the mystery of Nature enough?
Harnessing misfortunes into fortunes
Who the wizard is he?

85. In the Sea of Time

I want to dip into the sea of time
The vast hypothetical sea
Which capacities prolific voyage
To the navigators
But never seems to keep its promise
It is daunting to discover the new culmination
It is unmanageable to dip into it
For time is restrained into a slender hemisphere
Of a reduced radius
And in a world
Indefinable for man
Sometimes called the fourth dimension.

86. Confused Teen

The sweeping amend
I saw
Shivered me from top to toe.
I was astounded by the jealously
And self-interest of man
Man is mortal
So he ought to revert upon this fact that
The teen...
The confused teen should be secluded
Should be...
kept in stand still.
Nevertheless I qualified the true sense of being
I am drawn by a backward force
Which unable me to speak
Directly into the phizog of that ugly
Ill-behaved mortal
It's time now to labor under the roof
It's time now to labor under the roof (2)

87. A Dry Poem

My poems have dried up by now,
Unshakeable, immobile and uninteresting.
Days are dry now
Time is no less
Life has underwent a change to love autumn.
The poems of mine
Are fragile like the dry twigs...
And vanquished out like the tree tops.
No smile
Pale lovely sunken glow
Or
If not, at least a little hope
To see something prolific
By tomorrow.

88. Time -Time -Time!

Who rubbed against me?
The sadistic tie of time
Disabling me to be nostalgic,
Considerate and mournful
I wail on my fate
I howl on my misfortune
Someday ages and ages hence
I may savor the syrupiness of the fruit
Which I am leave-taking behind today...

89. Never Ending Race to Success!

Who says Success retards?

I say

Who says work hard and not waste time?

I don't say

For I myself is a fatality of success

Success in a course and

Not your Honey land

It is neither the destiny

Nor the pickup

It is an intermediate arrangement

Of delight, distress and nostalgia

Hence it is forever said

Wait for good jobs

And not for Success

For jobs will lead on the way to...

90. Fairyland

Where is the fairyland sited?
Please let me know
I want to retreat there
For the next summer...
Life is very daunting and exigenting out here
I can't prop up anymore torment
Let me recline for now...

91. I Missed It

Don't you assume I missed it all?
But the truth is that…!
I was a youngster and futile to apprehend
How crucial it was for me
I missed many stuff in my time
Probably you too…!
But life goes on
So does time
Never stop to turn back
Unless and until you want to be
A poet and a fantasist like me…

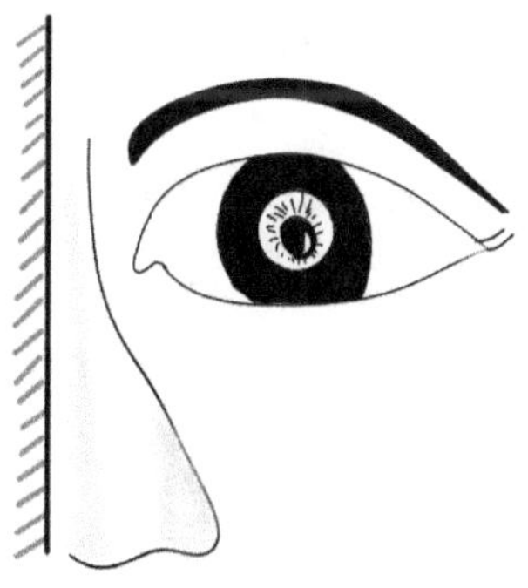

92. Why Are We So Indolent?

Be lazy......lazy....
Oh! Why are we so lazy?
I don't know
It seems I have been
Quiescent for an hour by now
Still I want to relax
Some more
The sun is blistering sharp and lucid
We must get on to our shoes
And dart to play about.
But I am so slothful
That neither me nor my brother
Desires to set out.

93. Wicked Things Approach

(Published in the Weaver Magazine)
We never worry when it lashes
Nor we worry when it's dark
Neither have we worried when it's piquant
As we all know
Everything that begins
Have to climax
So why do we agonize
When we face tough times
When we face strenuous situations
When we face repressive depressions?
You know it will edge
If not now than then
If not today than some day.

94. How the Diya Glimmers and Offs!

See dear, how the diya
How the diya glows and offs
It is rubbed with love and moisture
Then litted with a candle.
Kept away from blowing breeze
And protected from falling cascades
This diya will go off
Even after immense care
And devotion because
Even devotion has got its limit
Even love has got its end.
Life has got its dead lock
So try to cherries this very moment
This very diya.

MISCELLANEOUS

95. The Goddess of War

And who the nature reckons

On this auspicious gala of autumn.

A carnival of virtue over evil

Luminosity over blackness and

Verity over evility.

She comes like an

Auspicious mother and leaves

Us with soaked orbs.

And do you know what?

She does this every year

Standstill you ferocious wretch.

You have polluted our minds

Our lives and our sense of time.

You come in the form of Smartphone, laptop, i phones and what not

Come on let's celebrate this Festival and retreat to our

Old nostalgic days.

96. Krishna

Krishna you have melted my heart
With your authentic and attracting words
Your soothing voice layering your
Soft and piercing words
Can hypnotize even a leaf
An inactive rock can croon
And a hushed jungle can blossom into cerise
Your lotus eyes and yellow ware
Delights your pink cheeks
My blood will burst out of my veins
Only in your fidelity
You are an unsullied source of inspiration
For novices like this one
I entirely subdue myself on your petal feet
Krishna conduct me through this woods
Lead on my way to Bliss
Become my mentor, vicar and mate
You are not a material
You are an untainted soul of love and utmost devotion
My lamps have extinguished in your thoughts
And my imaginings have made you the protagonist
Of my theatre.

97. Stunning Diwali Isn't?

How gorgeous and fortuitous
Shall be the Diwali of 2020
In this era of Covid
We are despondent within
Our abode doors.
Will radiance come to us?
If yes, then when?
In this fete of Buoyant...
Festival of light
Where "light" subjugates "dark"?

98. Christmas

O the lord of the colossal sea,
The beau of mankind and serene
You stood in front of me
And, I know how I tingled
At that moment of pulse.
The world is sinking
Under its own adiposity
Of Shame, swindling and Crimes.
Its concretion has
Outweighed the buoyancy
Protect the saplings
Protect the passerine
Protect the wildlife
And if time permits
Protect mankind.

99. New Year Poem

I was sitting by my brother

When the hour hand bashed twelve

It's New Year, a fresh 2021

Is it truly the preliminary of a new era...?

Or simply a furtherance of Paucity, thoughtlessness and stuff.

I was unable to derive Mark Twain's Two important dates:

"The day when I was born

And the day when I realized why..?"

With this very plan

I headed bold to a novice instigation

As it is accurately alleged

"It's the right time to start now"

Hopes will never terminate

And once ended

Life shall be defunct.

100. Pen Pencil and So

Who did you asked?
About the gyrating pen
No one...
I am waiting for motivation!
What?! That's not the way
You must get stirred up from natura
From your deliverer
And if not than from your pencil
So!
So now get on your boots
And set off the marching
To the never ending race of eternity.

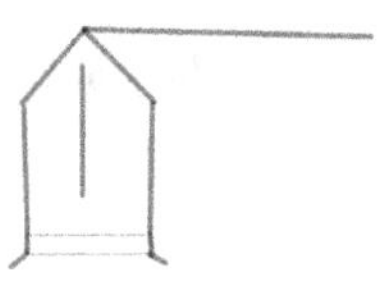

101. Wordsworth Frost and Shelly

These are not mere appellations

Of any great personality as you can imagine

They are beseeched souls

Who appeared and vanished

Like a Lockheed Blackbird

They hold the clout to civilize mankind

To arouse youth like this one

And to drudgery with keenness

For the triumph of Mankind

But by the way what is Success?*

We are the learners of other learners

And so my accolade to this three great gallant

Of their times

And also to those who not only

Shaped or sized the human race

But also augmented us with the honey

And sugar of Literature.

**Referring to the poem "__Never Ending Race to Success!__"*

102. The Ahoms of Assam

(A Tribute to the Great Ahoms)
Do you discern the famed
Ahoms of Assam?
Essentially they were not innate to this abode
They came from Yunnan
And migrated into Burma and Indochina
They are the ones with vigor, love and notion
They ruled for 598 years
And defeated the Mughals 17 times
They ruled from Charaideo
And set up a Paik system
Which sure-fired rights to
All the folkloric communities of their time.
Their cessation was dynamic and fascinating
They employed the treaty of Yandabo
Reassigning the knack to the British Sahibs
And accepting their fate with seclusion
This was a legacy they left
And this was all I could narrate

103. A Robust Women

(Dedicated to all women)
(International Women's Day)
And who she is
With a breezing smile
Invaluable, countless flattery cascade of hopes
She showers
She shoots her family, spree and bureau
She shields her homespun and children
She loves laughter in their face
And dreams livelier for all
She has a heart for all
And kindness has found its
Lodging in her
She is loftier than any obstacle
She is heftier than this Earth
She is a mother, wife, sister or daughter
Exultant International Women's day to all women.

104. Holi

Every iota of dye
Gives me the notion of gyrating
Around my mother, my family,
My state, and my nation.
The Nation's pride is solemnized
With hue of charm
O! The sumptuous vibes,
The aura of waft
That spells around my occult verity
Cavernously sketched
From my passion.

105. Not Ever Ending Jet

The jet of water flushes
Across my ends
Like the transient sand of any beach;
Like the winds of paradise;
Like the eras of central interstellar.
My life how much of it relics,
The night seems murky.

106. Granny's Pond

Granny's pond was chic
It was ancient and tranquil
But was quite special
For birdies and trawls
We sat beside it
In the daybreak and in the nightfall
Throwing shingles
Out of zealous and animosity.

107. Science and Literature

Science and literature goes
Hand in hand with
Not a single piece of disloyalty.
Science ratifies literature
While literature deepens science.
The amalgamation of both
Is what I seldom carve erstwhile.

108. Bihu

It is not a jubilee

It is a state of mind.

It is a rainbow of hundred colours

It is peace but in an altered form;

It is happiness in an infrequent shade.

So is Bihu

The pride and ecstasy of Assam

We all celebrate Bihu,

As a festival

But the veracity is that

It is only and only a state of mind.

109. Jules Verne

You made me tasteless
Your stories drift
Across my senses
Like frictionless brooks
And touch them by my heart.
I am a slave
Of overwhelming gushes
My life is a synopsis
Of all the consequences
Created in your novels.

110. Robert Frost

The way the floras
Of the hemlock tree
Changed your mood,
Your poems
Rehabilitated my behavior
Towards this stunning nature
Mother Nature vest in
The purest of the pure hearts
Somewhere ages and ages hence
Two roads will diverge in a yellow wood
And I shall take the one
Not trodden by many;
And that will make all the difference.

111. Isaac Newton

You produced many
You are a colossal entity
To this living universe
Your contribution is a
Mystic charm to all…
You are marvelous,
Hero of the five oceans
And seven lands
You made it to the same,
Principia Mathematica.

112. My Grandfather

(Dedicated to Mr. Mahendra Goswami)
You are a cradle of hope for me
An endless source of spur
Packed with hard work and dedication
You taught me to tenet this world
Not with power but with philosophies
You are a quartz pure stream of honesty.
Impetus has found its utopia in you
My grandfather,
I am indebted to you
For all your cascades of sanctifications.
I am a child and you are my grandfather. (2)

113. My Grandmother

(Dedicated to Mrs. Pori Goswami & Mrs. Manoroma Goswami)
The love star felt off from the divine sky
Just to touch this Earth in a human form
My grandmother,
You cared for me,
You are a benevolence indorsing complex
And generosity has touched its heights in you.
In you resides the keys of many locks
And when gladdened with devotion
Opens a thousand doors of mystery;
My life was one of them
And I am a child and you are my grandmother.

114. Workers are Not Only Workers

(With regards to International Workers' Day)
Who said workers are only workers?
They are a gift of heaven
They come for social good;
But return with lots of deterrence
You may treat them like engines
But always remember
There is also a worker
Somewhere within you
Who is keen to protect the dignity
Of these 'outdoor' workers.
Workers are not only workers…
Above all, they are humans
Just like you and me.

115. Tutankhamun

Who was Tutankhamun?
He was a boy king
Tough to explain
His life and
So is his death.
He was a ledge
Kept in the throne of Egypt
When Nefertiti
Was shining
It is the grandeur of Tut that now embellishes.

PROSE

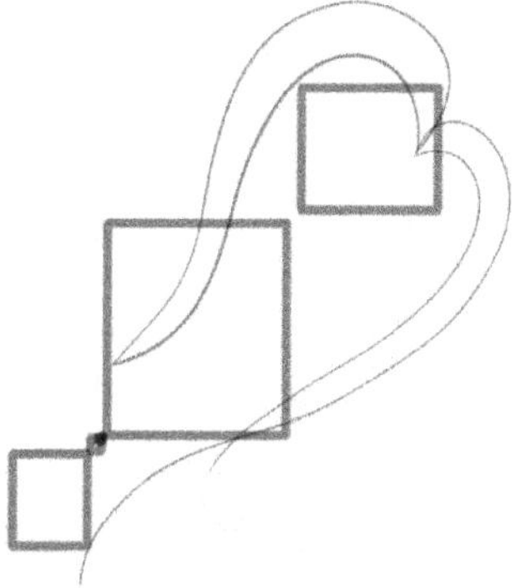

116. Time: A New Chapter

(Published in the Assam Tribune)

(Fetched "Contributor of the Week" Title)

*Miles Davis has said," Time isn't the main thing. It's the only thing."
This very statement motivated me to pick up the pen and pen down a few
worthwhile things which according to me must be heard by all students of
my age.*

*The value of time is best understood by the once who have already missed
it at some part of their life. Time for Students is like Diamonds for
Merchants who have not earned a penny or two since months. Interestingly
time is such an obsession which is received by all evenly irrespective of their
kind, creed, gender or even economic status. Then the question arises," Why
do some people run short of time while others sleep them out?" This serious
question invites many answers. One such answer can be people are defined
by the way they use their time.*

*I have seen many individuals wasting their time in pretty fruitless talks
and bits. So lastly I would like to keep my small opinion forward as, "If
you fool around your time today, then just make a mark, time will fool you
one day..."*

-By Hrishikesh Goswami

117. WHAT IS SMART WORK?

(Published in the Assam Tribune)
(Fetched "Creative Endeavour of the Month" title)

We all are quite household with the term hard work but very few of us actually acquaint themselves with the so called smart work. After a prolific research I came to know that fifty percent of the successful people did smart work and the rest fifty percent did Hard work!

So for the present generation it is awfully necessary to understand what exactly smart work is. Byron Dorgan has said, "Working hard and working smart sometimes can be two different things." Hence we must really know what to do and more importantly what NOT TO do! This will not only increase our chances of triumph but also will lead on to competence.

118. IDLE BRAIN: DEVIL'S WORKSHOP

I think we all are quite familiar with this idiom, right? And we should be. For me I once or twice experienced such a situation. The thing is that productive thoughts tend to keep people workaholic and so they don't even experience the powerful flow of time. It is often said, "Follow your heart but take your brain with you." For instance after exams or after the accomplishment of something great, we tend to relax for a while but this very relaxing tends to extend over a period of time destroying our priceless time and resources. Henceforth we must always keep an eye and an ear open to grad the opportunities life has to offer and not sit idle.

119. WORLD NO TOBACCO DAY

"Smoking leaves an unseen scar." "If you can't stop smoking, cancer will."
These are some of the often heard maxims when we listen to people with our
eyes, ears and minds wide open! Actually the depraved effects of Tobacco
are self-explanatory, the more you explain the more drastic they appear. In
simpler words I will say, "Tobacco Kills!"

But I know most of you will disregard me by telling that these are only
mere facts. I know this is because of the nicotine in that tobacco you
are smoking which is foiling you from staying yards apart from it. It is
purposely used by manufacturers to create a smoking cessation to relieve
withdrawal symptoms. Nevertheless it is not riotous to leave tobacco as
Tony Robbins said, "It is in your moments of decision that your destiny is
shaped."

QUOTES

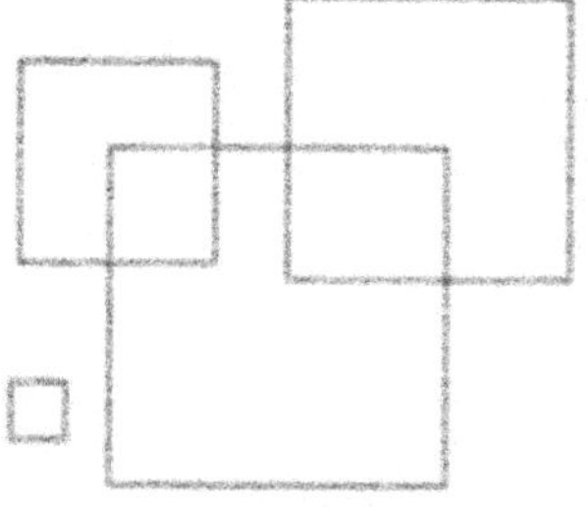

120. QUOTES

"To be or not to be: that is the question" -William Shakespeare

*"'Tis better to have loved and lost than never to have loved
at all" -Alfred, Lord Tennyson*

*"Two roads diverged in a wood, and I – I took the road less
travelled by" -Robert Frost*

"I wandered lonely as a cloud" -William Wordsworth

"Season of mists and mellow fruitfulness" -John Keats

121. COMMENTS ON POETRY

(From readers)

*Seven of Heaven commented on the poem **"Seasons"***
These lines express a wisdom, and perhaps a road to happiness, which is difficult to be achieved by many, including myself.

*Greatgaroo commented on the poem **"Seasons"***
It does seem that we are always in a hurry waiting for the next season, not taking time to enjoy the one we're in! Great description of rushing! God bless!

*Nunoftferreira commented on the poem **"Christmas"***
Wise and faithful words you have crafted and shared with a very smooth flow of all the lines...

*Butterfly4 commented on the poem **"Krishna"***
Beautiful poem, very well written. Nicely done

Dr. Ram Mehta commented on the poem "**Krishna**"
I am from Dwarika, where Lord Krishna ruled. Thanks for sharing the write.

Butterfly4 commented on the poem "**How the Diya Glimmers and Offs**"
Great poem, beautifully written, lovely theme, inspiring and heartwarming. Lovely

Iris3 commented on the poem "**Cohere the Water Rise**"
Awesome and significant
Nicely written

Chandra Roy commented on the poem "**Cohere the Water Rise**"
Nice one Clever write

Bronte44 commented on the poem "**Climber in My Balcony**"
Loved the poem. Represents hope and growth. Beautiful imagery.

122. CRITICAL ANALYSIS

Dear Hrishikesh,

I've enjoyed reading your poems ('Every Day is a New Challenge for me', 'Who is a Poet?' and 'Life in a Boat'). My initial thought is that a different approach to line breaks might help make the poems more dynamic. The poems you submitted tend to break at the end of a clause or a sentence, usually on a noun. When most of the lines end in that way, it quickly becomes monotonous for the reader. A solution might be to try varying your line breaks. If you ended on a verb, for example, the poem would gain some momentum as the reader would be driven to read on and find the object of the verb on the next line.

Secondly, sometimes the poems seem a little distant and abstract. I think they would benefit from more specificity, perhaps using content from your own life. For example, in 'Every Day is a new Challenge', I wanted to know what kind of work morning brings you. A good example of a poet who uses specific instances from their own life is Eileen Myles. Their poem 'Snakes' might give you some ideas for how to integrate specific details into your own poetry.

I hope this feedback is useful to you. Obviously, you know your own poetry better than I do, so feel free to ignore any comments you disagree with!

Good luck with your writing and best wishes,

Tom.

(Sent on behalf of all the editors: Monique, Tom, Tawseef and Hannah.)

Fruit Journal

Manchester (UK)

E- PLATFORMS

According to me E-Platforms are often proved to be the best stages to showcase talents and inert abilities. Dear Readers after reading this small probationary of mine I request your kind perusal over the listed social platforms.

123. YOUTUBE

SCAN THIS QR CODE

124. LINKS TO ALL OTHER PLATFORMS

https://linktr.ee/hrishikeshgoswami

About The Poet

(World Record Holder) (India Book of Records Holder for Poetry) (Creative Endeavour of The Month April 2021 by The Assam Tribune) (Recipient of India Prime Top 100 Author Award 2022) (Recipient of India Star Icon Award 2022)(Author of The Year 2021 Nominee) HRISHIKESH GOSWAMI is a Contemporary Naturalistic poet from Assam, India who specialises in writing about nature and realism coalescing fiction and non -fiction in a sophisticated blend. Author of The Poet's Words, The Secret: Nature Reveals, Poems for Poets, The Exegesis, 72 Haiku, 51st Tanka, The Sesquipedalian Notion along with Co-Author of World Record Anthology Book – "Bilingual Aesthetics" and editor of the E-Poetry Anthology 'The Euphoric Verses from Soul' and the Literary Anthology 'Forest & Me' and 'The Idiosyncratic Mystery'. Hrishikesh Goswami fell in love with writing from a fledgling age of 14 when he was at the 9th standard. Hrishikesh Goswami's poems have been featured in The Assam Tribune, Blue Lake Review, Indian Poetry Review, the Weaver Magazine, Poets India, Soul Connection brought up by Guwahati Grand Poetry Festival, Anthology Still I Rise brought out by Wingless Dreamer, Winter Poems Anthology brought out by Poets Choice. Hrishikesh Goswami has been highlighted by Media Houses such as India Saga, Daily hunt, Spot Latest, Fox Story India, Glamwist etc. Hrishikesh Goswami has also been interviewed by Fox Story India and published in their Magazine. Hrishikesh Goswami is also available in E platforms like Story mirror, Anchor, Spotify, Wattpad, Google Podcast, Apple Podcast, Breaker, Pocket Cast, Radio Public, All Poetry, Listen Notes, Poetry Soup, Commaful, Hello Poetry, SoundCloud, Poem Hunter etc. for his dear readers. Readers can find further information about the poet in Google and YouTube by typing "POET HRISHIKESH GOSWAMI " for the same.

Hrishikesh Goswami has been bestowed with Certificate of Commendation in Never Such Innocence International Poetry Contest, Certificate of Achievement from Asian Council for English Proficiency Test conducted under CAFLR norms, Certificate of Merit for Outstanding Performance in NationWide Mega Science Experiment Conducted by NCERT, VVM, VIBHA and Ministry of Education, Govt. of India, Editor's Choice Award in International Essay Writing Competition by

Monomousumi and is recognised by World Record University, Career Development College London, Guwahati Grand Poetry Festival, WWF India, APJ. Abdul Kalam International Foundation, ASSIST WORLD RECORDS, PONDICHERRY BOOK OF RECORDS and Royal Commonwealth Society. He has been two times State Level Tae-kwon-do Champion, Gold Medallist of several National and International Competitive Exams and Olympiads, a KVPY Scholar, Winner of National School Level Essay Writing Contest conducted by Maulana Abul Kalam Azad Awards 2020, Grand Master of Mental Arithmetic-Senior A Whole Brain Development Program from Aloha (Abacus), Visharat in Hindustani Classical Music, Best Debater of PRARAMBH 2021 conducted by Nehru Group of Institutions, Kerala, Holder of Honourable Mention in several notable Poetry Competitions and has been Featured in Top 20 Leaderboard of International Science Film Festival Quiz 2021.

Apart from these Hrishikesh's poems have been critically analysed by Fruit Journal

Manchester (UK), Acorn (A journal of contemporary haiku), The Leading Edge Magazine, BreakBread Magazine and has been published by The Assam Tribune's Horizon and Planet Young, NEZINE (An online magazine), Noverse Foundation and FoxGales Publishers, Poem hunter-The World's Poetry Archive, Cultural Reverence (An International Digital Journal Of Art and Literature), Tech Touch Talk of Kolkata.

Hrishikesh Goswami's poems have been read by The Liminal Review, Poetry London, The Tether's End, Tears in the Fence Literary Journal, *MASKS Literary Magazine,* Ribbons, *The Hopper* (An environmental literary magazine), The West Trade Review, Split Rock Review, The Baltimore Review, Rollick Magazine, The Poetry Magazine, Chestnut Review, The Sun Magazine, The Society of Classical Poets, The Greensboro Review, The London Magazine, TheKenyon Review, The Adroit Journal, Washington

Square Review, Wilderness House Literary Review and many more. Hrishikesh's haiku poem has been translated into Japanese and published in a traditional Japanese style literary anthology.

Nevertheless Hrishikesh's poems have been able to gratify the minds of critics to an extent and hopes to improve this range in the upcoming years. A few of his poems have also been widely accepted in Poetry Circles and Forums.